Lebendiges Englisch 1

That's Entertainment

Eine Lektüre zum Gebrauch
nach Lektion 15,
Lebendiges Englisch Band 1.

Max Hueber Verlag

Herausgegeben von James Aller und Yvonne Whiteman
Bearbeitungen von James Aller

CIP-Kurztitelaufnahme der Deutschen Bibliothek

Lebendiges Englisch. – München [i.e. Ismaning]: Hueber
Teilw. bearb. von Hans G. Hoffmann
NE: Hoffmann, Hans G. [Bearb.]
1.
Lektüre 2. That's entertainment : e. Lektüre zum Gebrauch nach
Lektion 15, Lebendiges Englisch Bd. 1 / [hrsg. von James Aller u.
Yvonne Whiteman]. – 1. Aufl., 1. Dr. – 1983.
ISBN 3-19-312191-6

1. Auflage

| 3. 2. 1. | Die letzten Ziffern |
| 1987 86 85 84 83 | bezeichnen Zahl und Jahr des Druckes. |

Alle Drucke dieser Auflage können nebeneinander benutzt werden.
© 1983 Orlando Language Texts Ltd, Bath
Gesamtherstellung: Sulzberg-Druck GmbH, Sulzberg im Allgäu
Printed in Germany
ISBN 3-19-312191-6

Inhalt

Pantomime (George Speaight) 4
Twiggy Talks About The Press (Twiggy) 8
The Play At Mansfield Park (Jane Austen) 10
The Art Of The Monologue (Joyce Grenfell) 16
Anglo-Saxon Type No. 2008 (David Niven) 18
Entertainment In The 20s (Yvonne Whiteman) 22
Fred Astaire & Ginger Rogers In Top Hat (P Jenkinson) .. 24
Fred Astaire Talks About Top Hat 26
Passing The Time In Hospital (Josephine Tey) 27
The Archers (Norman Painting) 30
The Auditions (Noel Streatfeild) 32
Good Performances (J B Priestley) 35
Michael Winner At Work (Bill Harding) 38
Incidents (Lillie Langtry) 40
In Uniform (Peter Ustinov) 44
The Lamentable Comedy (William Shakespeare) 47

Word List 51

Acknowledgements .... Umschlagseite 3

Pantomime

There exists in Britain – and only in Britain – a unique and extraordinary kind of theatrical entertainment. Intellectuals usually take no notice of it, but it is very popular with the general public. In provincial cities, it attracts large audiences of rather unsophisticated theatre-goers – the kind of theatre-goers who probably never go to any other form of theatre in their lives. It is basically a traditional kind of theatre; but over the centuries it changes continually, just as popular taste changes. People usually think of it as entertainment for children; but you will often hear risqué jokes in it that only their parents can understand. People often say it is dying, but it never does die. It is the Christmas pantomime.

Wherever you go, the basic structure of a pantomime is generally the same. When the curtain goes up, a fairy comes on the stage from the right, waves her wand and announces the story in rhyming couplets. Sometimes it's about a giant who terrorizes the land, or a magician who is planning something terrible, or an awful uncle who wants to carry off his wards. Whatever the story, the fairy announces that she will stop the evil and protect the good.

But there then comes on the stage from the left, in a green spotlight, a demon king or a bad fairy. He or she announces ruin and terror, and says a few more awful things in rhyming couplets. The audience doesn't hear these, because by then it is hissing and booing – the audience knows exactly what to do, and when.

The second curtain then goes up. Behind it is a market place or a village green, or perhaps a street in old Peking. We see people from the village dancing and singing; or often there is a special number by a troupe of children from the local dancing school.

There comes on then a very surprising figure: a man in women's clothes – the Dame. He (she) takes no notice of the story. Instead, he takes up a position at the front of the stage. (Here a microphone often replaces the footlights now.) He begins to "warm the audience up". Probably the first thing he does is to welcome the parties who are visiting the theatre for that performance – the Little Muggins Women's Institute, the St Stephen's Church choir etc. At each name, the party he is welcoming announces its presence with a loud cheer.

The Dame then asks the boys and girls if they are enjoying themselves. They always answer with a loud, uncritical "yes" and his answer is "Well, you should leave now, because it gets worse later on". Then he begins to tell them some jokes which have little (or nothing) to do with the story.

It is surprising perhaps, but true, that the audience always laughs loudly at these jokes. But it is time for the next main character to come on. This time it is a girl in tights and trunks. She plays the part of a man – the Principal Boy. She (he) then sings a song, usually a popular love ballad of the season; soon another girl comes on and joins her – a real girl this time. She may be a princess, or a woodcutter's daughter, or a pretty, perplexed youngest sister. The main thing is, she is certainly in love with the Principal Boy.

The story then begins to get underway. It may be *Cinderella*, *Jack and the Beanstalk*, *Aladdin* or *Dick Whittington*, *Robinson Crusoe* or *Babes in the Wood*, *Mother Goose* or *Puss in Boots*. There are only about a dozen well-known stories in the pantomime repertory. But, to tell the truth, it doesn't really matter what the story is – somehow a number of well-tried, traditional scenes will always be there.

One of these will be a chase. On the stage will be two doors and a window. The guards or policemen chase the Dame – she runs out of one door and in at the next, so quickly that soon she is chasing them; and then she disappears down the hole in the floor and jumps out of the window. And you realise that there are two, if not three, Dames.

Another favourite scene (but you don't see it so often now) is a "slosh scene". In this, the characters throw custard pies or wallpaper paste in each other's faces. The victims then sit on their hats, or walk in the glue pot or fall into the bath.

Or there may be a funny motor car that falls to pieces with a lot of noise and steam and explosions. Or the bailiffs come and take the furniture out of the Dame's house; or the scene is a Chinese laundry in *Aladdin*, where someone pushes someone else into a mangle, and the second person comes out as thin as a piece of paper. The Dame probably finds an excuse to take off her clothes, and we see layers of petticoats and corsets and red drawers. She comes on stage again carrying a long, long washing line across the stage. On the line are the most improbable underclothes in the colours of the local football team. She goes off to the right, and then surprisingly appears again at the end of the line, from the left.

During all this, the audience play their part, and shout "Look behind you" when a skeleton appears or a spider comes down from above on the end of a line. Or they take part in an unending dialogue of "Yes, you did" and "No, you didn't," with someone on the stage.

And somewhere or other, a travelling troupe of acrobats or circus dogs appears, or golliwogs dance a ballet, or we see beautiful scenery. In one recent show, it was a pop group or a television star. And of course, there's always a horse or a cow or a goose with actors inside.

Between all this, the story thinly makes its way until someone kills the giant, or saves the babies, or puts the glass slipper on to

Cinderella's foot. Then comes the "song scene": a big cloth comes down on the end of a line, on it the words of a popular song. The Dame encourages everyone to sing it – sometimes she divides the audience into two groups, who sing against each other.

After this, the cloth goes up again, and we see behind it a colorful scene with some steps in the middle. All the characters walk down it in their most beautiful costumes, the least important character first and the most important character last. The most important at the end are the Principal Boy and Girl. And we all clap and cheer, and somebody makes a speech saying, "If you enjoyed the show, tell your friends. If you didn't, keep your mouth shut."

George Speaight

Twiggy Talks About The Press

I know what to do at interviews now. I should be able to – after so many interviews. But at that time I was just seventeen, and it was all so new to me. I didn't even think that anybody would be clever or nasty with me, and I needed Justin [Twiggy's boyfriend/manager] near me. That's why he got such a reputation – people thought he didn't give me a chance to speak. It wasn't even that I was so naive. Once I was just getting off a plane in Minneapolis and was giving a press conference. A reporter asked me straight out: "Twiggy, what do you think of sex?" There was a terrible silence, and I just wanted to curl up in a hole. In private I didn't find it a problem to talk about the subject, but I certainly didn't intend to speak out in public about such a personal matter. Justin stepped in and told the reporter it was a silly question and he was wasting my time. Now, after so many interviews and talk shows, and so many tricks that people tried, I know what to do myself, and I don't have to talk about it.

When I was in America, the press really had fun with me, all their clever writers ... They called me an "elongated matchstick", "the original million-dollar baby doll". The magazine *Seventeen* said, "It's like watching poetry. She is Harlow, Garbo, the boy next door." I was on the cover of *Newsweek*. There was an enormous photo of my face in *Paris Match*: "Garçon ou fille? Non! C'est Twiggy!" (Boy or girl? No! It's Twiggy!) I liked to see the photos of myself on all the news-stands, but I didn't read too much of the long pieces they wrote about me in the papers. They were always trying to analyse why I was successful, or writing great long studies of my character.

There were a lot of image-building things about me, too. Often they mentioned the fact that I didn't drink or smoke, and I always went to bed early. Most of that was true – I do smoke, in fact, off and on, but always just two at a time, and then perhaps the next, two weeks later. I never particularly liked the taste of alcohol. And as for early to bed, well, I was still very young and I worked very hard during the day, and I don't like crowds. So I never went to nightclubs; I still don't.

It wasn't that I was very self-conscious. I didn't think to myself, "Wow! This is all happening to *me*!" I was so busy with my work; and although it all happened to me very quickly – it was literally overnight success – I was just working, doing the thing I loved most: modelling clothes. The personality thing was just something that happened on the side. I didn't do anything to get a particular image. The press made a lot out of things that were just a part of my character. I was lucky that they wanted to write about me ...

I didn't find it easy to answer questions, I must admit. I just answered everything spontaneously. When they said people were exploiting me, I said that might be true – I hardly knew what "exploit" meant. Anyway, I didn't mind, because people were being lovely to me. It was all as if I was reading about someone else, though. I really was sincere in everything I said, and people found it surprising that I wasn't a super-sophisticated "swinger". I said I missed my mum and dad most of all because it was true. I really did miss them. I wasn't a fraud. I didn't believe everything I read about myself, so I didn't get big-headed. There were whole-page adverts in the *New York Times*, advertising the TV films about me. And they interrupted radio programmes every five minutes, just to say what Twiggy is doing *now*. How could anyone take that seriously?

Twiggy

The Play At Mansfield Park

[At the Bertram family's large house in the country, Mansfield Park, family and guests decide to organise a play. At first, everyone is enthusiastic. But then problems begin to come up. Fanny Price, who is Lady Bertram's niece and is living at Mansfield Park, watches it all.]

Everything was now under way: the stage, the actors, actresses and costumes were all going well. But, although no other great problems came up, Fanny found after a few days that it was not all pleasure for the people who were taking part.

Everyone began to find difficulties. Edmund had many. Wholly against his advice, someone sent to the town for a painter, who was now at work on the scenery. This was not only very expensive – it did nothing for their morale. Edmund's brother Tom Bertram refused to listen to him when Edmund said it was going to be a private performance. Tom was giving invitations to every family he met. Tom himself began to worry about the scene-painter, who was working very slowly. Tom already knew his part, in fact, all his parts, and was getting impatient. (He was doing all the other little parts that the Butler could do.) He wanted to start acting. Day after day went past when they did nothing, and he began to feel more and more how unimportant all his parts were together. He was beginning to be sorry that they were not doing some other play.

Fanny was a good listener. Often she was the only person who would listen to anything. She heard all their complaints and dissatisfactions. *She* knew that everyone thought Mr Yates shouted too much; that Mr Yates was disappointed in Henry Crawford; that Tom Bertram spoke too quickly and no-one would understand him; that Edmund wasn't learning his part; that it was terrible to have anything to do with Mr Rushworth – Mr Rushworth had to have a prompter through every speech. She also knew that nobody wanted to rehearse with Mr Rushworth; she had to listen to *his* complaints about that, as well as everyone else's. In fact, it was obvious to her that her cousin Maria was avoiding him. Instead, she was having unnecessary rehearsals of the first scene with Mr Crawford. Soon Fanny was afraid that she would hear all sorts of other complaints from *him*.

It was not the case that everyone was happy and was enjoying himself. Far from it. Everyone wanted something he did not have, and this made everyone else unhappy. Everyone had a part which was too long or too short. No-one was on stage when they should be; no-one remembered which side they had to come on stage; people complained that no-one else did what they should.

Fanny expected that she would get as much simple pleasure from the play as any of them. Henry Crawford acted well, and it was a pleasure to *her* to creep quietly into the theatre and listen to the rehearsal of the first act. This was pleasant despite the feelings which some of the speeches stirred up in Maria. She thought that Maria acted well, too – perhaps too well. After the first rehearsal or two, Fanny was the only person who stayed to listen. Sometimes as prompter, sometimes as audience, she was often very useful.

As far as she could see, Henry Crawford was by far the best actor of them all. He had more confidence than Edmund, more judgment than Tom, more talent and taste than Mr Yates. She did not like him as a man; but she had to admit that he was the best actor. On this point, there were few who would not agree with her. Mr Yates, it is true, said in a loud voice that Crawford was rather colourless. And the day came at last when Mr Rushworth turned to her with a black look and said, "Do you think there is anything very fine in all this? Upon my life, I cannot admire him. Between ourselves, it is quite silly that a mean-looking man like that should call himself an actor."

From this moment, his old jealousy of Crawford came back. Maria had growing hopes of Crawford, and made no effort to do anything about her fiancee's jealousy. It became less and less probable that Mr Rushworth would ever know his forty-two speeches. The idea that he might make a success of them occurred to no-one except his mother. She, in fact, was sorry that he didn't have a larger part. She stayed away from Mansfield until they were a long way forward with the rehearsals and she could see all his scenes. The others only hoped that he would remember his cue and the first line of his speeches. The prompter would help him through the rest.

Fanny was sorry for him, and tried very hard to teach him how to learn. She did everything she could think of, and even made an artificial memory for him. She herself learnt every word of his part; but in the end he did not get much better.

Fanny had many moments when she felt uncomfortable, of course; but there were very many things that needed her time and her attention. She was very useful to them all, and had a lot to do. Her first worries were in the end unjustified. And she was perhaps at least as happy as any of them.

There was of course a lot of work do on the costumes, and here she could help. Mrs Norris had no doubts about it: "Come on, Fanny," she said, "it's all right for you, but you mustn't walk from one room to the next and just watch everyone else. I want you here. Here I am, working so hard that I can hardly stand. I'm trying to finish Mr Rushworth's coat without buying any more materials. You can help me put it together. *You*'ve got the best situation, I can tell you. But if no-one did more than *you*, we should not get very far."

Fanny took the work very quietly, and did not try to defend herself; but her kinder aunt Bertram said for her: "It's nothing unusual if Fanny is enjoying the excitement, sister. It's all new to her, you know. Once upon a time, you and I were very fond of plays ourselves. Certainly I still am. As soon as I have a little more time, I am going to look in at their rehearsals. What is the play about, Fanny? You never told me."

"Oh, sister," said Mrs Norris, "don't ask her now. Fanny isn't one of those who can talk and work at the same time. It's about two lovers."

"I believe," said Fanny to her aunt Bertram, "there will be a rehearsal of three acts tomorrow evening. You will have a chance to see all the actors at the same time."

It did not worry Lady Bertram that she had to wait until the next day; but Fanny did not feel at all comfortable. In those three acts, Edmund and Miss Crawford would act together for the first time. There was in the third act a scene which interested her particularly. She longed to see the performance, but at the same time she was afraid. The whole subject of it was love: the gentleman would describe a marriage of love, and the lady would practically make a declaration of love.

***

The first real rehearsal of the first three acts was going to take place in the evening. Mrs Grant and the Crawfords said they would come back as soon as they could after dinner, so that they could take part. Everyone was waiting for the evening. A spirit of cheerfulness was in the air. Tom was pleased with the progress on the play. Edmund was in a good mood after the morning's rehearsal, and all the little problems seemed to disappear. Everyone was impatient to see the play. The ladies went out, and the gentlemen went after them. Soon, everyone except Lady Bertram was in the theatre. They were only waiting for Mrs Grant and the Crawfords before they began.

They did not wait long for the Crawfords, but there was no Mrs Grant. She could not come. Dr Grant said he was ill, and could not do without his wife.

Here was a disappointment! What bad luck that Mrs Grant could not be there. She was such a pleasant and delightful person when she was with them, and she always agreed with everyone. And now they absolutely needed her. Without her, they could not act and could not rehearse. The pleasure of the whole evening was over. What could they do?

Tom, the Cottager, was in despair. After a silence, eyes began to turn towards Fanny. A voice or two said, "Perhaps Miss Price could *read* the part." At these words, everyone surrounded her, everybody agreed, even Edmund said, "Please do, Fanny, if you don't find it *too* unpleasant."

But Fanny still refused to come forward. The idea was terrible. Why didn't they ask Miss Crawford as well? She thought she should go to her own room – there she would be safe. Better to be there than at the rehearsal – she knew it would be awful. Why did she come? Now here was the punishment.

"You only have to *read* the part," said Henry Crawford again.

"I'm sure she can say every word of it," added Maria. "The other day she corrected Mrs Grant twenty times. Fanny, I'm sure you know the part."

Fanny could not say that she didn't. And, as they all went on asking her, as Edmund said it again with such a look at her, she accepted. She would do her best. Everyone was happy – and they left her alone with her beating heart while they began to get ready.

They *did* begin — and they were too busy with their own noise to hear an unusual noise in the other part of the house. They were already quite a long way into the first act when the door of the room flew open, and Julia was standing there. Shock was on her face as she said, "My father is here! He is in the hall at this moment!"

(From **Mansfield Park**)

The Art Of The Monologue

When interviewers ask me: "Where do I get ideas for my monologues, an easy answer is, 'If I knew, I would go there again.'" When I was young, I had a photographic and aural memory for details. I remembered clothes and the expressions on people's faces, as well as accents and things that people said. I have a theory that I was an observer probably until I was twenty. I put everything into my memory, and am still using it.

Now I am more interested in what people are thinking – and why – than in their funny hats and the funny things they say. I can no longer tell you the colour of their eyes or their ties, or whether they have moustaches and plucked eyebrows. But I do still notice voices and speech mannerisms ... Some of the people of my age who write plays, and who had their biggest successes when they were young, no longer seem to listen to how we speak now; though their dialogue may be about the ideas of today, their talk echoes an older style of speech. Nothing is sooner out-of-date than everyday speech.

A writer once asked me what audience I had in my mind when I wrote monologues. She said *she* wrote her books with the image of her worst enemy looking over her shoulder. When I was working on material, I never thought of an audience at all. If I could not entertain myself, I didn't think I could hope to entertain anyone else. When I began, I found it amusing when people were silly, snobbish, humourless, pompous or heartless. Now I am more interested in people as individuals. Perhaps I am more tolerant now; or possibly I become bored more quickly.

One occasion excepted, I don't believe I ever sat down to write a monologue. I always knew the character I was looking for, and how it showed itself in voice and accent. It was the voice that gave form to the character; with it instinctively came mannerisms and movements. I talked aloud to myself as I moved about the flat, thinking myself into the style of the creature which I was trying to bring to life. Sometimes I imagined backgrounds – bedrooms, clothes, tastes (if any). The story itself was the last thing I thought about. As I built it all up (this took anything from two days to a month), I quickly wrote down keywords and expressions, and so the piece came together. Only then did I write it out in full.

One character appeared one night when I was cleaning my teeth. I looked in the mirror and curled back my upper lip, so that I could make sure they were clean. (My teeth are as large as tombstones, and are therefore noticeable. It is practical to keep them in good order.) It then occurred to me that here was a new face: how would it speak? It spoke in a clear, brusque, educated way, and what it said was short and to the point. I went into the living room where Reggie [my husband] was still reading, and I said, "This is my new monologue face," and talked to him in the new voice. He liked it. In my gallery of "monstrous women", she is my favourite character: the wife of an Oxbridge vice-chancellor. She has no name, but I know her well. I admire her intellect and her wit, and I love her generous assumption that everyone else is as well-read and well-informed as she is. There is not much of me in this lady. I wrote three short pieces about her called "Eng. Lit." [English Literature].

(From **Joyce Grenfell Requests The Pleasure**)

"Anglo-Saxon Type No. 2008": a film extra in the 1930s.

With its usual efficiency, Central Casting called me to my first job as a professional actor – as a Mexican.

In area, Los Angeles is one of the largest cities in the world. Most of the film studios are in strategic positions in the suburbs, a long, long way from the centre. Universal Studios is in the San Fernando Valley. They said I should be there at 5 a.m. The Auburn [my car] broke down the evening before, so I started a zigzag journey across the city by street car at 3 o'clock in the morning.

When I arrived at the studios, the man at the gate put a piece of paper in my hand through a small window. It said I should go to Wardrobe. I waited in line, showed my paper (which they stamped), and got a baggy white suit, a large sombrero, some sandals and a blanket.

I changed into my new clothes in a huge, barn-like dressing room. Other "Mexicans" were also putting on their outfits. "Indians" were also getting ready, and honest townspeople were getting into tailcoats, top hats and bowlers. The women "extras" were dressing in the barn next door.

I went with my fellow "Mexicans" to the make-up department, where, once again, we stood in line. Those of us who, like me, have fair skins, had to stand while they sprayed our faces and hands with a brown mixture. On others of us they glued moustaches.

The "Indians" in the line opposite were getting the same treatment, except that they were spraying them all over with a red mixture. Somewhere, they were doing the Chinese in a yellow mixture.

There wasn't much happy conversation, I noticed.

At six-thirty, an assistant director came along and pushed us all into buses. We drove for one hour to a movie ranch, where the permanent Western town stood. There, other assistants told us where to stand and when to move slowly, when to run in alarm, etc. The cowboy star (whoever he was) arrived, and at eight o'clock precisely they started shooting. The director's name was Aubrey Scotto. He did not bother with us. It was a harassed assistant who pushed us around all day.

At one o'clock, they gave us a cardboard box, and said we had half an hour to eat. Inside the box were a piece of chicken fried in batter, some cookies, an orange and a small packet of milk. After lunch, we started shooting again, until the sun was too low and the light too weak and we couldn't go on.

During the last scene, the extras pushed and pulled a lot, just to make sure that they were "established". Only then did the studio call you back automatically the next day.

Back at the studios, I waited in line until I could get to the washbasin and wash off my make-up. I handed in my moustache and clothes and they stamped my paper again. Then there was a last long wait at the cashier's office before I could show my paper and collect my money.

Fortunately there were a group from Hollywood who were going back by car, and I went with them. But even so, it was ten o'clock before I sat down in the drugstore and waited for my "50 cents Blue Special". My money for my first day as a professional actor was two dollars and fifty cents.

***

These were the golden days. The movie business was booming. The studios were making hundreds of films every year, and there wasn't much competition from other forms of entertainment. Television was not even on the horizon. Night football and night baseball were in the future. No-one played bingo or went bowling.

This was the age of the Great Stars. The Supreme Court's anti-trust decrees were still in the future, and the newspapers still had several pages each day with nothing but Hollywood news and gossip in them.

The studios looked to the future, and carefully built up their teams of favourite stars. When I worked in crowds at Metro Goldwyn Mayer, I often stared in awe at the names on the dressing room doors ... Garbo, Norma Shearer, Jean Harlow, Joan Crawford, W C Fields, Wallace Beery, Spencer Tracy, Hedy Lamarr, William Powell, Myrna Loy, Louise Rainer, Robert Montgomery, Lionel Barrymore, John Barrymore, Charles Laughton and the Marx Brothers.

The supporting actors were a powerful lot, too: Frank Morgan, Louis Calhern, Robert Young, Franchot Tone, Reginald Owen, Lewis Stone, H B Warner. And the "babies": some of them did their school work in little cubicles on the sound stages. Under Californian law, they had to do a certain number of hours each day ... Elizabeth Taylor, Mickey Rooney, Lana Turner, Judy Garland and Ava Gardner. They were all under contract to one studio at the same time.

Other studios had their stars, too. At Warners, it was James Cagney, Pat O'Brien, Edward G Robinson and Bette Davis. At Paramount there was Gary Cooper, Charles Boyer, Claudette Colbert and Marlene Dietrich, while at RKO Fred Astaire, Ginger Rogers and Cary Grant were supreme.

It is no surprise that young people with stars in their eyes came to Hollywood from all parts of the world. There was hardly a beauty contest winner anywhere who didn't book a hopeful one-way ticket.

No surprise ... outside Central Casting ... "DON'T TRY TO BECOME AN ACTOR. FOR EACH ONE WE EMPLOY, WE TURN AWAY A THOUSAND." And it is no surprise that, behind Hollywood shop counters, or working as car hops and waitresses, or selling theatre tickets, swimsuits, ice creams or their bodies, were the most beautiful girls in the world.

(From: **The Moon's a Balloon**)

Entertainment In The 1920s

In 1922, the British Broadcasting Corporation (the BBC) started to broadcast programmes over the "wireless" (i.e. the radio) from Marconi House in London. Soon, almost every schoolboy knew how to make a simple "crystal set" which could pick up the programmes.

Jazz was the other sound craze of the 20s. In 1919, the Dixieland Jazz Band came over to Europe from New Orleans and played in London for the first time. They introduced listeners to the exotic atmosphere of Harlem, with numbers like *I'm Forever Blowing Bubbles, Alice Blue Gown* and *Tiger Rag*. The Bright Young Things were wild about the new musicians – they called them *divine*, *super* and *king*. Soon you could hear nothing but jazz, jazz, jazz everywhere you went. Thanks to the Dixieland Jazz Band and a successful new review called *The Blackbird* (with its hit song *Bye Bye Blackbird*), negroes and Harlem culture were suddenly fashionable. Because of this exciting new music, people call these years "the Jazz Age" or "the Roaring Twenties".

If you wanted to be fashionable, you trailed a cloud of cigarette smoke behind you, from a long cigarette-holder. Every fashionable woman smoked, although only a few years before, even the idea of it was unimaginable. From America there came the idea of the "cocktail hour": people began to drink strong alcoholic drinks with names like the *Widow's Kiss* and the *Maiden's Blush*. A new word came into the world: the *hangover*, which described the awful effects of drinking too much. Everyone made jokes about it (but not many people made jokes about the Young Things who went further in their experiments and became miserable drug addicts).

Most evenings, after they came out of the latest revue in London's West End, the Bright Young Things went to a night club — perhaps to the *Midnight Follies* at the Hotel Metropole; or they went to have dinner and watch the *Piccadilly Revels* at the Piccadilly Hotel.

Or they simply went to the Trocadero. Here they jumped around and learnt the latest dances: in 1922 it was the Foxtrot, in 1923 the slower Blues. From 1926, the Charleston was the craze which hit Europe. Everyone wanted to dance like Fred and Adele Astaire. Clubs and hotels employed professional male partners called *gigolos* or *lounge lizards*. Rich women without partners could hire them as dancing partners. (After the War there were many rich women without partners.) These professional partners were usually Latin American or Southern European and were quite good-looking in a dark sort of way. Their clothes were cut to "swooning point" (as one observer said), with "padded shoulders and mermaid hips".

(From **Looking Back at Fashion 1901–1939**)

Fred Astaire & Ginger Rogers In Top Hat

With *Top Hat*, Fred and Ginger finally became top stars. The film had its first showing on 16th August 1935, and people now think of it as the definitive Astaire/Rogers musical. One important advantage is that it has a lot of great tunes by Irving Berlin, including *No Strings*, *Isn't It A Lovely Day?*, *Cheek to Cheek*, *The Piccolino* and, of course, the memorable title song.

As in *Roberta* before it, Hermes Pan's name appeared as the choreographer, and the polished direction was by Mark Sandrich, whose experience was in slapstick. The sets were a triumph, with wonderful modern, art deco and Venetian scenery.

In his solo number *No Strings*, Fred does a sand dance, in which he throws the contents of a large ashtray over the floor of his hotel room – this is to deaden the sound. In *Isn't It A Lovely Day?*, the couple find themselves together in a bandstand during a rainstorm. They do a fast dance routine around the limited space of the bandstand. The number is a masterpiece of timing and precision; but their most romantic dance of all is *Cheek to Cheek*. During the dance, Ginger's lovely feather dress and Fred's usual dress suit blend beautifully with the music of Irving Berlin.

In the *Piccolino*, the scenery is more traditional, and you can see the pattern of the choreography more easily. Even so, it is the weakest number in an otherwise almost perfect film.

The high point of the film is the *Top Hat, White Tie and Tails* routine, which is better than anything that Astaire did before it. It is an all-time classic of music and dance. He rehearsed the routine for almost two months, and gave all his attention to the complicated routines, until they were perfect. His professionalism paid off.

The sound engineers did their part, too. The rat-tat-tat of Fred's feet, echoing the sound of a machine-gun, form a noisy staccato against the restrained sound of the orchestra.

As usual, Van Nest Polglase created wonderful false perspectives and Venetian-style scenery, but in the end it was Astaire himself who danced his way to film immortality, putting on his Top Hat.

Philip Jenkinson

Fred Astaire Talks About Top Hat

Top Hat was a good picture. I think it's a kind of standard that doesn't really age very much. It's just timeless. As long as you know that people will show it for a long time, it's nice that it still seems good. I always loved that film.

Ginger had this dress with all kinds of feathers on it and, you know, they started to fly. They just dropped, and every time we started the dance, the cameraman said several times a day, "Wait a minute, wait a minute, the feathers, there's a feather in Mr Astaire's ear" or something. Or there was a feather in front of Ginger's nose. So we always stopped, and I said, "All right". And this happened so many times that we couldn't get that dance.

In the end the dress became a little used and the feathers got looser, and in the end it looked like a snowstorm. So we had to wait until all the loose ones got out of the way. There were so many feathers on this dress that I guess some of them had to go!

And in the end we did get the number. Actually it's always a good topic of conversation now, but I didn't think so at the time, I can tell you.

(From the **Fred Astaire Story**)

Passing The Time In Hospital

[Inspector Grant is in hospital, and is very bored.]

He heard someone come across to his bed, and he shut his eyes – he did not want to talk. He did not want either sympathy or briskness just now. In the pause that followed, a faint enticement played with his nostrils and swam about his brain. No, it wasn't the little nurse – she smelled of lavender. The big nurse smelled of soap and iodoform. The expensive smell that was playing with his nostrils was L'Enclos Numero Cinq. He knew only one person who used L'Enclos Number Five: Marta Hallard.

He opened one eye and looked up at her. She was standing as if she did not know what to do – she thought he was asleep. She was looking at the pile of obviously unopened books on the table by his bed. In one arm she was carrying two new books, and in the other a great pile of white lilac. She looked very handsome, very Parisian, and wonderfully unhospital-like.

"Did I wake you up, Alan?"

"No, I wasn't asleep."

She dropped the two books beside the others.

"I hope you find these more interesting than the others. It seems you didn't find any of them interesting."

"I can't read anything."

"Is your back painful?"

"Agony. But it's not my back."

"What then?"

"It's what my cousin Laura calls 'the prickles of boredom'."

"Poor Alan. And how right your Laura is!"

She picked some flowers out of a glass that was much too large for them. With one of her best theatrical gestures, she dropped them into the washbasin, and in their place put the lilac.

"You think boredom is a great emotion, but it isn't. It's a small, silly thing."

"Small nothing. Silly nothing. It's like an attack of nettles."

"Why don't you take up something? You could study one of the philosophies. Yoga, or something like that."

"I thought I would go back to algebra. I never did algebra justice at school. But I've done so much geometry on that ceiling up there that I'm not really keen on mathematics just now."

"How about crosswords? I could get you a book of them, if you like."

"God forbid."

"Do you play chess? I don't remember. How about chess problems?"

"My only interest in chess is pictorial."

"Pictorial?"

"The pieces are very elegant, you know."

"Oh. I *could* bring you a chess set to play with ... All right, no chess. You could do some academic investigating. That's a sort of mathematics. Find a solution to an unsolved problem."

"Crime, you mean? I know all the case-histories by heart. And I certainly can't do anything about them."

"I don't mean things from Scotland Yard. I mean something more – what's the word? – something classic. Something that was always a problem."

"Like what, for example?"

"Mary Queen of Scots's letters?"

"Oh, *not* Mary Queen of Scots?"

"Why not?" asked Marta. Like all actresses, she saw Mary Stuart through a haze of white veils.

"I could be interested in a bad woman, but never in a silly one."

"*Silly*?", said Marta in her best Electra voice.

"*Very* silly."

"Oh, Alan, how can you!"

"It's the headdress that seduces people. That's the only reason people are interested in her."

"You mean, in a sunbonnet she loved less greatly?"

"She never loved greatly at all, in any kind of bonnet."

Marta looked as scandalized as a lifetime in the theatre allowed.

"At least she was a martyr. You must agree there."

"A martyr to what?"

"Her religion."

"She was a martyr to rheumatism, nothing else."

"In a moment, you'll say she was not a prisoner."

"Your trouble is, you think of her in a little room at the top of a castle, with bars on her window and one old man to wait on her. In fact she had more than sixty personal servants. When they took 30 of them away, she complained bitterly. And when she had only two secretaries, several women, a cook or two and one or two others, she nearly died. And Elizabeth had to pay for all that out of her own purse! For twenty years she paid, and for twenty years Mary Stuart offered the crown of Scotland round Europe to anyone who would start a revolution and put her back on the throne. Or the throne that Elizabeth was sitting on."

He looked at Marta and found that she was smiling.

"Are they a little better now?" she asked.

"Are what better?"

"The prickles."

He laughed.

"Yes. For one minute I completely forgot about them. At least Mary Stuart has that to her account."

(From **The Daughter of Time**)

The Archers

Few radio programmes have as many friends and as few enemies as *The Archers*. As always over the last 30 years, it tells the story of everyday country people.

When the programme began, much of English life was different from today. There were very few television sets in homes, while the number of radios was more than 12 million: for every TV set there were 30 radios. Not many families had cars; even fewer had two. Fridges were still luxury articles, and home-freezers were unknown. Most homes did not have washing machines or washing-up machines.

On farms, many farmers still milked their cows by hand and used horses for the ploughing. Air travel was for the few – and hijackings were unknown. The two great popular entertainments were the cinema and the radio, although variety theatres and music-halls still had good audiences, although they were smaller than before.

Britain still had a complete system of steam railways. You found central heating mainly in public buildings or very big private houses, and double-glazing was uncommon. Travel in space was still a dream. Food rationing was an everyday reality.

It was into this grey, post-war world of shabbiness and shortages that *The Archers* came. It brought with it a glimpse of a life that had the same shortages, the same restrictions and frustrations – but it was a life that seemed less grey, more full of hope. The sun shone brighter there, the grass was greener.

The public gave the programme a warm welcome. A few weeks after it began, it was already a favourite with listeners, and very soon it was more than that. For many, the characters in Ambridge were real people. Their lives made them more real than reality – their lives were certainly more meaningful than many of the daily lives of our listeners' own families, friends and relatives. In Ambridge [the town where *The Archers* takes place], farmers are now milking the cows for the 26,001st time, the population is drinking its 20,001st cup of tea and its 12,001st pint of beer. The signature tune *Barwick Green* is enjoying its 28,001st playing on the radio, but it still remains fresh.

From the first, *The Archers* seemed more authentic and real-to-life. The explanation for this is simple: from the first, the programme used the imagination of its listeners.

Who were these new characters who, after a very short time, were names which were known in every house, in every part of the country? Basically, they were at first one family, with one or two friends. Dan Archer, the patriarch, was a good tenant-farmer – honest, hard-working and with a lot of problems. His best friend was the lovable but feckless Walter Gabriel, who represented the bad, inefficient farmer.

As a necessary change of scene – and also so that we could hear comments from time to time – there was the village pub, with its regular drinkers. In the series, it was necessary to have someone or something who represented town life, who could draw parallels, make contrasts and ask simple questions in a natural way. No countryman asks (for example) "Why do you dip sheep?" or "What do you use a harrow for?" A townsman does – and did.

As long as the programme continues to avoid both the trivial and the fashionable, remains honest and convincing; as long as it continues to include the lasting things of human life and love and death, *The Archers* itself will last. And we will continue to see things like this (which comes from a West of England newspaper): "Wood for sale. Call any time (except during *The Archers*)."

(From **FOREVER AMBRIDGE**)

The Auditions For A Midsummer Night's Dream

The stage was full of people, most of them adults. Petrova [Pauline's sister] was glad that she could stand behind the other students, out of sight. She could not even face the thought that, soon, she would have to go out in front of everybody and dance. It made her feel funny inside, when she just thought about it — as if she were eating an ice-cream too quickly. She thought, too, that it was going to be a waste of time. Nobody would want to engage as a fairy a child who had a stye on her eye.

The audition began with a lot of people singing. They sang uninteresting songs, mostly in German and Italian, and the children were bored. The songs seemed to go on for hours and hours. Then suddenly a voice called from the stalls: "Pauline Fossil". Pauline got up quickly. Her nanny pulled her skirts straight, and Pauline ran down to the footlights. She stood there, while a lot of people talked in low voices. Then, because nobody told her what they expected from her, she put up her hand because of the glare from the footlights and looked for the person in the front row ... At that moment, the man at the far end of the row stood up and called out, "Can those children who are auditioning for the part of Moth please come forward?"

The two girls from the Academy, and a boy from another school, came to the footlights. Mr French pulled down the tip-up seat next to him, and asked Pauline to sit. A large man with a cigar, who was standing on the other side of Madame, spoke first. He said that he thought it was a good idea if they had a boy for the part. Madame said she thought her girls would look better. In the end, they asked the boy to say his piece. He said "Prospero's Epilogue" quite well, but with a very ugly accent.

"A pity about that voice," said the man with a cigar. "Clever boy. Could have understudied Puck."

They all looked round at a man in the row behind. They asked if the boy's voice was always as bad as that, or was it nervousness? The man said nervousness, he thought. Someone suggested that they hear a few separate words out of the play. They asked the man to ask the boy to say "hail". The men went to the front of the stalls and leant across the orchestra pit.

"Say 'Hail', Peter."

"Hile," said Peter.

"No. Hail Hay-Hay-Hay-el."

"Hile," the boy said again.

All the men in the stalls looked at each other and shook their heads. The man with the cigar told the man in charge of Peter that it was no good. He asked Madame to bring on one of her girls. Both of them came forward. One did a speech by Titania and the other did a piece of poetry. Pauline liked the Titania speech best, but they engaged the one who said the poetry. They then called for the Cobwebs. Four girls came forward, all with red hair. One of them, who was not from the Academy, was much smaller than the others. They asked her to recite. She was not very good, but her accent was all right, and they engaged her. Then they asked for Mustard-seed. There was a pause. Then the girl who was going to be Cobweb curtsied to Madame and said, "She isn't here." It was then that Pauline had her big idea. Why couldn't Petrova be Mustard-seed? She pulled at Mr French's sleeve.

"My sister is here. She would be a very good Mustard-seed." He looked at her in surprise, and said that he did not know that she had a sister. Anyhow, they wanted a dark Mustard-seed.

Pauline explained that Petrova was dark, and said please would he have a look at her.

To Petrova, that walk from her chair at the back of the stage to the footlights was about the worst thing in her life. Behind the footlights sat all those terrible people. Her feet felt large, her hands clumsy and her stye seemed the largest in the world. When she got to the front of the stage, things got worse. Leaning across the orchestra pit was Madame. In her nervousness, as she curtsied, Petrova fell over. All the children on the stage tittered. Red in the face, she got up.

Her "m'audition" was "the boy's speech from Act III, Scene ii, of *Henry the Fifth.*" Everything went wonderfully until she reached the end of the part that describes Pistol. She knew that the next bit was about Nym, but she could only remember the words "For Nym ..." Desperate, she looked round for inspiration. As she did so, Pauline came to her rescue. She knew the speech perfectly. She slipped out of the stalls and into the stage-box. This was close to Petrova's left ear. She leant forward.

"'For Nym'," she prompted, "he hath heard that men of few words are the best men".

As soon as Petrova saw Pauline and heard her prompt, she not only remembered the rest of her speech, but said it far better. It was wonderful how good it was that she was so close to her, close enough that she could touch her.

After Petrova finished, Pauline went back to her seat, and Petrova stood there, feeling awkward again. She did not have much time to feel awkward. Almost at once, Pauline came flying through the pass door, her eyes shining. She pulled Petrova into a corner.

"We've got them. We've got them. We've got them. They're engaging both of us – me for Paeseblossom, and you for Mustardseed."

(From **BALLET SHOES**)

Good Performances

Miss Trant returned to the Pavilion earlier than usual in the evening. Although, as usual, it was drizzling mournfully, which made the Pier look more forlorn than ever, crowds of people were already moving along towards the Pavilion. At almost the last moment, Sandybay was discovering that *The Good Companions* were offering it an unusually good show. Ten minutes before the beginning of the performance, all the unreserved seats were full, and a number of people were standing at each side and at the back. Five minutes later, after the theatre managers pushed a few more people in, they put up a "House Full" notice, and they were actually turning money away ...

The whole atmosphere of the place was different. You knew at once that, on the other side of the curtain, there weren't any cold spaces any more, no empty chairs and yawns and slow stares. Everybody was expecting a delightful evening's entertainment; everybody was ready to accept anything that the players did, and was only waiting for the moment when they could hum and laugh and break into storms of applause. Miss Trant tried hard to stay calm, and to find amusement in the excitement of the others, but she couldn't. Her excitement was as great as theirs, and she was only glad that she herself did not have anything to do. Oh, it was perhaps absurd, but it was thrilling, it was fun!

The lights went out and the footlights came on. Applause already. Then – one, two, three, and the music began. *Rumty-dee-tidee-dee. Rumty-dee-tidee.* Quietly at first, then louder, louder. Then they let it rip. You could feel the whole house as it moved with its rhythm through the curtain. They were tapping; they were humming; they were eating and drinking it. A final triumphant phrase, as Jimmy crashed his drumstick against the cymbal. A moment's silence. Then the Pavilion seemed to be full of clapping hands.

"Put the instruments away," shouted Jimmy through the noise. "Everyone on stage for the opening chorus. Come on, come on. All right, Inigo? Ready with that curtain, Oakroyd? Gosh! It's going with a bang tonight!"

And with a bang it went. They clapped when Joe warned them against the mighty deep, and clapped again when Mrs Joe discovered Angus Macdonald as he was coming home from the war. They rose like a storm when Elsie sang that she was looking for a boy like them. The welcome for Morton Mitcham was so great that they would not let him go, until in the end he was just sweat and grinning bone. He did so many tricks and played so many tunes that his cards and his strings were probably burning at the end. Each time Jimmy opened his mouth or crossed the stage, they roared with laughter. And when Jerry Jerningham did his "slipping round the corner", and Susie brought out her new song about "going home", they had no mercy. They clapped, and stamped their feet, and whistled and drummed their feet time after time, to bring the two of them back again. When the final curtain came, it was nearly eleven o'clock – three-quarters of an hour after the usual time. Even then, the audience would not stop clapping. "Spee-ee-eech!" some of them were calling.

"Ladies and gentlemen," Jimmy began.

That was the signal for more clapping. In the middle of it, the attendant pushed his way up to the stage, in his arms a large bouquet of roses. The lights came on, and everyone on stage could see that bouquet of roses as it came nearer. The three women never took their eyes off it. Mrs Joe was not without her hopes – could there not be a Music Lover in the house? Elsie thought that probably there was a gentleman friend – Elsie was rich in gentlemen friends – in the front row. Susie was already preparing a special smile and curtsy – it was hardly possible that the bouquet was for anyone else.

The attendant held up the bouquet, and Jimmy came forward with a jump, and took it from him. He read the note, and the three women held their breath. He turned, and with a funny gesture and an ironic smile, gave it to – Jerry Jerningham.

Mr Jerningham, very warm, very tired, a little shiny, perhaps, but still exquisite, bowed his thanks very gracefully. Then, after quickly looking at the note, which said "To Mr Jerry Jerningham, from an Unknown Admirer" in a fine, feminine handwriting, he smiled again at the audience, and smiled at his fellow players. Three of them were trying to hide their expressions of amazement and disgust.

(From **THE GOOD COMPANIONS**)

Film Director Michael Winner At Work

One veteran actor, the late Robert Ryan, said this after he worked with Winner on *Lawman*:

"He does things in a radically different way. Every other director of my acquaintance follows more or less the usual method – they film the whole scene, using all the actors in what we call "master shots". They then move to medium shots, close-ups, and so on. Winner doesn't work that way. In fact, in this picture we didn't make any master shots. He does something different – we call it "cutting with the camera". This means that you only shoot scenes which you are going to use. It has one disadvantage – at least to us older actors. In this case, we have to rely on Winner's camera technique to give what we call a "sustained performance". But I'm quite willing to see the results."

Winner shoots wholly on location – he hates the artificially of studios. "Life doesn't take place in studios, it takes place in real places," he says. It is a philosophy which takes him to dangerous places – the ghetto areas in the United States, for example. This is where Americans are afraid to get out of their cars, but not one determined Englishman.

Winner doesn't plan his films shot by shot. He thinks that it forces actors into a fixed scheme; and this doesn't help the actors to give believeable performances. In his philosophy, when you are on location, the filming which you do in the first hour suggests what you put into the second hour. What you do in the first two hours suggests what you put into the third, and so on through the day. Although the scriptwriter always prepares the script as well as possible, Winner does not mind if he has to change things at the last minute. Like Antonioni, he often lets the camera run on after the end of a scene. Sometimes he catches the players off-guard, and many of the shots of laughing actors or confusion are included in the final film. Often, Winner finds that he does not need to take more than two "takes", and he rehearses only if the actors ask him to rehearse. He finds that the best performances usually occur during rehearsals, which means he is not able to film them.

On location, the atmosphere of a Winner film is famous for its good humour, but from time to time there are flashes of bad humour which cause tension. He is impatient. He knows what he wants and how he can get it. And, although he often says it is not true, he is ruthless with anyone who seems weak, or who won't do what he tells him, or forgets to do so. "It's a team when a lot of people do what I say." He knows that the success or failure of each film depends on the final result – it doesn't depend on the crew's opinion of him. It can be a disaster for a film if the crew tells the director what to do. But although Winner is tough, his crews stay with him. Year after year, you see the same names in the credits. They respect his technical knowledge, and he respects those who work hard. From personal experience, he knows how easy it is for something to distract a writer. Sometimes he locks his writers up until he is satisfied with their screenplay.

(From **THE FILMS OF MICHAEL WINNER**)

Incidents From The Life Of A Famous Beauty

It was one evening late in June, at a supper at the house of Sir Allen Young, the Arctic explorer, that I met His Majesty King Edward, at that time Prince of Wales. Sir Allen loved his friends – he was hospitable and popular, and one of His Royal Highness's frequent hosts. Everyone called him "Alleno".

There were about ten of us at this party, and we were all waiting for supper. I did not know at all that such an important guest was coming to supper, and I was wondering why we were waiting. Suddenly there was a stir outside, then everyone in the room fell silent. Sir Allen went out quickly, and soon I heard a deep, cheerful voice: "I am afraid I am a little late." Sir Allen said something polite as an answer, and the Prince of Wales appeared in the door.

Obviously he was on his way from some important occasion, because he was wearing several orders and the blue ribbon of the Garter. He looked round the room, and shook hands with the women when they curtsied and the men as they bowed – he knew all of them there. Only my husband and myself were new to him. It so happened that I was standing by the fire when Sir Allen came forward and presented me to His Royal Highness.

I was in a panic. For one moment, I thought I could try to escape by climbing the chimney; but then I realised that this was silly. I stood where I was, and curtsied. After this, my husband suffered the same agonies as he bowed, and I rather enjoyed watching him.

At the supper table, I found myself sitting next to the Prince. However, when he said something, both my husband and I could give only monsyllabic answers. But, although I said little, it was very interesting to watch the Prince. I soon realised that, while he was good-humoured and pleasant with everyone, he kept his dignity very well. It would be a brave man who tried to be familiar with him.

* * *

When I met Oscar [Wilde], he was fresh from Oxford, where he won the prize for the best poem of the year, called "Ravenna". He was very modest about his success, and I heard of it from other people. Soon other beautiful verses started to come from his pen, and it was then that I became the inspiration for one of his best poems. The poem, with a dedication to me, is included in Oscar's first volume. He presented me with a white leather-bound copy in which he wrote:

"To Helen, formerly of Troy, now of London."

Before Oscar became famous, he always brought me flowers, but he did not have enough money for large bouquets. When he came to visit me, he came through Covent Garden flower market on the way, where he bought me a single, lovely amaryllis. After this, he walked down Piccadilly to my house, with the single flower in his hand. People thought this was all an act, and so they called him "the Apostle of the Lily".

... When he was writing *The New Helen*, he became obsessed with the subject. For hours at a time, he walked round and round the streets in which our little house stood. He was probably, in his mind, giving me all sorts of qualities that I did not have. Although Wilde had a wonderful sense of the ridiculous, he was sometimes almost ridiculous himself. For example, one night he went to sleep on my doorstep, and when Mr Langtry came home very late, he put an end to Oscar's poetic dreams by falling over him.

It was for me that Oscar wrote *Lady Windermere's Fan*. I cannot think why he thought this would be a good play for me at the time – and I never thought of him as a dramatist, anyway. He came to our house one afternoon with an important expression on his face and a manuscript in his hand. He put the manuscript on the table, pointed to it with a dramatic gesture and said:

"There is a play which I wrote for you."

"What is my part?" I asked. I was not sure if it was a joke or not.

"A woman," he answered, "with a grown-up, illegitimate daughter."

"My dear Oscar," I answered, "am I old enough to have a grown-up daughter of any sort? Don't open the manuscript – don't try to read it. Put it away for twenty years."

***

The king who came to visit us most often in those days was Leopold, King of the Belgians. Paris and London were his playgrounds. He enjoyed himself in these capitals in the most democratic way. He walked about in the streets quite alone, and visited his friends, in London at least, at all times of the day or night.

One morning, for example, at nine o'clock, the butler knocked on my bedroom door (I was still upstairs), and said that His Majesty the King of the Belgians was here and was waiting in the drawing room. This was a great surprise to me. I put on my gown in a great hurry and went downstairs. There was His Majesty, wet to the skin, with a wet umbrella in his hand – he came on foot from his hotel. I curtsied, as was polite, and sat down. I wondered what he would say to explain this early visit. But he did not think it was necessary to explain it, and for a long time we sat and made rather uninteresting conversation. He was wearing his usual formal clothes, but on this occasion, at this time of day and in this weather, they looked rather ridiculous. The next day he came at exactly the same time, and this time I excused myself politely.

***

I signed a contract for my first American appearance in the coming autumn. In a great hurry, I got together all the clothes and other things that I needed for my tour. I must say I was not very enthusiastic about the tour at the time. The United States seemed to me about as far away as Mars, and about as difficult to get to. Everyone now knows how the States were a delightful surprise to me, and I made America my second home.

My opening night at the Park Theatre was going to be only a few days after my arrival in New York. In between, we used the time for rehearsals.

On opening night, I left the theatre and returned to the hotel about five o'clock. I felt comfortable – everything was completely ready. Perhaps half an hour later, Pierre Lorillard ran into the room, his voice full of excitement: "I am afraid that the Park Theatre is on fire!" And it really was. From my window I could see the building which carried all my hopes. Flames were bursting through the roof. There was a great crowd of people in the street. They were there to see me, but now they turned their attention to the burning building. In the light from the fire we could see the whole of Madison Square. It seemed that the only thing which would escape the fire would be the large sign high over the roof, with my name – "Mrs Langtry" – on it. I stood and watched that sign. It seemed to me that my fate depended on it. "If it stands, I shall succeed!" I said. It started to fall. "And," I said, "if it burns, I shall succeed without it!" *But it stood!!*

The building burned down completely. Sadly, two people died, and the fire destroyed all the costumes except mine.

The next day the papers said that the fire at the Park Theatre was the biggest and most expensive advertisement for a play ever seen in America.

(From **THE DAYS I KNEW**)

In Uniform

In this atmosphere, it was not I who began to crumble but my stomach. They sent me to a military hospital for observation. Here, they ordered complete rest for me, in a part of the hospital which looked out on to the playground of a lunatic asylum. Through the window, I could see, at all times of the day and night, old ladies crying like peacocks and lifting their clothes over their heads.

They said that my complaint was due to nerves, and sent me to a man whom they called a Personnel Selection Officer. In fact, his role was to find me a job which was suitable to my inclinations. That was the theory, at least. In practice, it was rather different. The man was Scottish, and (rather unusually) had a very black moustache and short, snow-white hair. He looked like a very bad print of Groucho Marx at the height of his success, only he was much less charming, less funny and, in the end, less human.

He said he had looked at my case, and asked me how much money I earned as a civilian, before the War.

I said that I was self-employed, and the money would be different each week.

Patiently he asked the question again, as if I were a rather slow-minded colonial.

"It's not difficult to understand," he sang in his tuneful Scots voice, "I just wanted to know what you earned every week in time of peace."

I told him that I understood his question, and would try to make my answer just as simple.

"Since I am an actor and a writer, I do not have regular employment. Very often, I earn nothing in a week." I tried to laugh, but he did not laugh with me. "When I do earn something, it is of a variable or inconsistent sort."

He closed his eyes. It seemed he was trying to find a hidden store of patience. He breathed deeply.

"I don't know why you are making this difficult," he murmured. "I just asked you how big your pay cheque is at the end of every week."

"And that is just the question to which I cannot give a precise answer," I replied in the same clenched voice. "You must know that actors sometimes have a bad year. Well, a bad year means that there are more bad weeks than good weeks. As you will understand, I cannot give you the average of good and bad weeks. I do not have a long enough history."

He sighed, and looked up at the ceiling, as if something unusual was happening there. I did not look up, because I knew that nothing interesting was happening there.

"Let me ask you the question in a different way," he said after a while. "If it were now peace time, how much would you earn this week?"

At this point, I had a wonderful idea.

"If you like, sir, I can tell you how much money I shall earn this week."

He closed his eyes and broke a pencil.

"I know how much you will earn this week," he moaned, as if he were near to tears. "You are a private soldier in His Majesty's Armed Forces. I *know* how much money you will get this week!"

"But you do not, sir," I said. My fourth play *The Banbury Nose* was in its first week at Edinburgh. The reviews were very good, and I had already got my first royalty cheque. I looked at a piece of paper. "Last week, I earned eighty pounds, seventeen shillings and four pence, my army money not included."

45

He banged on the table with his fist, and jumped to his feet. "You're lying!" he screamed.

I explained the facts of the case. I hoped that he would be less angry if I mentioned Edinburgh. Perhaps he was from Glasgow – in any case, it did not make things better.

"Right," he said, looking darkly across the table. On the table was one of those simple games which psychologists use. Young children can do them easily. "Right, these are my conclusions. It is clear that film-writing is not a suitable activity for you psychologically. I am sending you as a clerk to the Royal Ordnance Depot in Donington Park. It will be your job to grade underwear in sizes –".

I did not listen or hear any more. For once in my life, I lost my temper. I picked up the game and threw it to the floor. The Scotsman backed to the door in alarm, and called for help. Two Military Policemen came and took hold of me, and in a hurry took me to the psychiatrist, who was a female colonel.

I told her sarcastically what had happened. She was sensitive to my sarcasm, and laughed. She brought me a cup of tea, and told me I should not worry. In a week or so, they were sending me to a part of the army which specialized in entertainment.

I went back to my hospital room and watched the people in the lunatic asylum again. There were, as always, much worse situations than mine.

(From **DEAR ME**)

The Lamentable Comedy

Act 1, Scene II. Athens. A room in QUINCE's house. or a [Enter *Quince, Snug, Bottom, Flue, Snout* and *Starveling.*]

Quince	Is all our company here?
Bottom	You should call them all, one by one, according to the script.
Quince	Here is the list of characters. On it is the name of everyone who we consider suitable to act, through all Athens, in our play for the Duke and Duchess on his wedding day at night.
Bottom	First, good Peter Quince, say what the play is about. Then read the names of the actors, and let us get on.
Quince	Well, then. Our play is called, The most lamentable comedy, and most cruel death of Pyramus and Thisbe.
Bottom	A very good piece of work, I assure you, and very funny. Now, Peter Quince, call out your actors from the script. Gentlemen, stand back, please.
Quince	Answer when I call you. Nick Bottom, the weaver?
Bottom	Ready. Tell me what part is mine, and go on.
Quince	You, Nick Bottom, are down for Pyramus.
Bottom	What is Pyramus? A lover? Or a tyrant?
Quince	A lover that kills himself most gallantly for love.
Bottom	That will need some tears in the true performance of it. If I do it, the audience must watch for their eyes. I will cause storms; I will show grief. For the rest ... yet I am in the mood for a tyrant. I could play Hercles wonder-

fully, or a part to storm and rage, and break the world in pieces:

The raging rocks
And shivering shocks
Shall break the locks
   Of prison gates:
And Phibbus' car
Shall shine from far
And make and mar
   The foolish fates.

That was sublime! That was Hercles's style, a tyrant's style. A lover shows more grief. Now name the rest of the players.

Quince	Francis Flute, the bellows-mender?
Flute	Here, Peter Quince.
Quince	You must do Thisbe.
Flute	What is Thisbe? A famous knight?
Quince	It is the lady that Pyramus must love.
Flute	No, no I cannot play a woman. I shall have a beard soon.
Quince	That does not matter. You can use make-up, and you can make your voice as high as you like.
Bottom	If I can hide my face, let me play Thisbe too. I'll speak in an awfully high voice. Listen, my lover's voice: "Thisne, Thisne!" My high voice: "Ah, Pyramus, my dear lover; your dear Thisby, and dear lady!"
Quince	No, no you must play Pyramus; and Flute plays Thisbe.
Bottom	All right. Go on.
Quince	Robin Starveling, the tailor?
Starveling	Here, Peter Quince.
Quince	Robin Starveling, you must play Thisbe's mother. Tom Snout, the tinker?

Snout Here, Peter Quince.
Quince You play Pyramus's father. I shall play Thisbe's father. Snug the joiner, you play the lion's part. And there, I hope, we have all the parts.
Snug Is the lion's part ready? If it is, please give it to me because I am a slow at learning a part.
Quince You can improvise it. It is nothing but roaring.
Bottom Let me play the lion, too. I will roar so that it will be a pleasure to hear me. I will roar so that the Duke will say, "Let him roar again, let him roar again."
Quince If you did it too terribly, you would frighten the Duchess and the ladies, and they would all sream. That would be enough to hang us all.
Everyone That would hang us, every mother's son.
Bottom I agree, friends. If we frighten the ladies out of their minds, they would have no choice. They would have to hang us. But I will change my voice and roar for you like a baby dove. I will roar for you like a nightingale.
Quince You will play no other part but Pyramus. Pyramus is a sweet-faced man; as good a man as you will ever see on a summer's day; a most lovely, gentleman-like man. Which means you must play Pyramus.
Bottom Well, I will do it, then. Waht beard should I have?
Quince Why, any beard you like.
Bottom I can perform in a straw-coloured beard, or perhaps an orange-coloured beard, or a red beard, or a French royal beard.
Quince Some of your French royal heads have no hair at all, and then you will play beardless. Now, gentlemen, here are your parts. I must ask you, no, I will beg you to learn them by tomorrow night. We shall meet tomorrow night in the palace wood, a mile outside the town,

	in the moonlight. There we will rehearse. If we meet in the city, we shall have people all around us, and then everyone will know what we are doing. In the meantime, I will make a list of things that we shall need for our play. Please do not forget to come.
Bottom	We will come, and in the wood we shall rehearse more boldly. Work hard; be perfect. Goodbye.
Quince	We shall meet at the Duke's oak, then.
Bottom	Enough! Keep the appointment, or be disgraced!

(From A MIDSUMMER NIGHT'S DREAM)

Word List

absurd absurd
accent Akzent
accept zustimmen
according gemäß dem
account (to her) (auf ihre) Rechnung
acquaintance Bekanntschaft
acrobat Akrobat
act Schauspiel
act Akt (Theater)
act spielen (theat.)
act schauspielern
actor Schauspieler
actress Schauspielerin
admire bewundern
admirer Bewunderer
admit zugeben
adult (n) Erwachsener
advantage Vorteil
advert Werbung
afraid ängstlich
age (the ... of) das Zeitalter der
age (v) altern
air Luft
alarm (in) (voller) Bestürzung
all over überall
all-time (adj) noch nie erreicht
allow zulassen
although obwohl
amaryllis Narzissenlilie

amazement Erstaunen
amusement Vergnügen
announce ansagen
antitrust decree monopolfeindlicher Erlaß
anyway sowieso
appear erscheinen
appear as auftauchen als
appearance Auftritt
armed forces Streitkräfte
army Armee
art deco Jugendstil
article Artikel
artificiality Künstlichkeit
as so (wohl als auch)
as als, für
as for was betrifft
as well as sowohl als auch
ashtray Aschenbecher
asleep eingeschlafen
assistant director Regieassistent
assumption Annahme
assure versichern
atmosphere Atmosphäre
attack Angriff
attendant Diener
attention Aufmerksamkeit
attract anziehen
audience Publikum

audition Hörprobe
audition for sich einer Hörprobe unterziehen für
aural Hör ...
authentic authentisch
avoid vermeiden
awe (in) voller Ehrfurcht
awful schrecklich
awfully schrecklich
awkward ungeschickt

baby-doll Babypuppe
back (v) sich zurückziehen
background Hintergrund
bad luck Pech
baggy ausgebeult
bailiff Gerichtsvollzieher
bandstand Musikpavillon
bang (with a) mit einem Knall
bang on hauen auf
bar (n) Gitter
barn-like scheunenartig
baseball Baseball
basic Grund ...
basically grundsätzlich
batter (n) Teig
beard Bart
beardless bartlos
beat (v) schlagen
beauty contest Schönheitswettbewerb
beg anflehen
believe glauben
bellows-mender Blasebalgmacher

beside (prep) neben
big-headed eingebildet
bingo Bingo (Lotteriespiel)
bitterly bitter
blanket Decke
blend with sich vermischen
blow bubbles Seifenblasen machen
boldly dreist
boom (v) blühen
bored (be) gelangweilt sein
bored (become) sich langweilen
boredom Langeweile
bother with sb. sich abgeben mit jmd.
bouquet Strauß
bow (v) sich verbeugen
bowler Melone (Hut)
bowling Kegeln
brain Gehirn
brave tapfer
break down kaputt gehen
breath Atem
breathe atmen
bright (adj) hell
bright young thing die jungen Engländerinnen
briskness Lebhaftigkeit
broadcast (v) senden
brusque kurz gefaßt
build ... up entwickeln
building Gebäude
burst through durchbrechen
butler Diener

camera technique Kameraführung
capital (n) Hauptstadt
car hop Bedienung im drive-in-Restaurant
cardboard Pappe
careful sorgfältig
case (n) Fall
case-history Fall-Geschichte
cashier's office Kasse
catch sb. offguard unbeobachtet aufnehmen (Schnappschuß machen)
cause (v) verursachen
ceiling Wolkenhöhe; Decke
central casting Vermittlungsstelle f. Schauspieler
century Jahrhundert
certain sicher
chance (a ... to) eine Gelegenheit zu
character Rolle, Person
charge of (in) verantwortlich für
charming charmant
chase (n/v) Verfolgungsjagd, verfolgen
cheer (n) Freudenruf
cheerful freudig
cheerfulness Heiterkeit
chess Schach
chess set Schachspiel
chimney Schornstein
chinese laundry Chinesische Wäscherei
choir Chor
choreographer Choreograph
cigarette-holder Zigarettenspitze
cinderella Aschenputtel
civilian bürgerliche Person
clap (v) klatschen
clean (teeth) putzen
clenched (adj) gepreßt
clerk Angestellter
clever raffiniert
close (v) schließen
close to nahe an
close-up Großaufnahme
cloth Tuch
clothes Kleider
cloud (n) Wolke
clumsy plump
cobweb Spinnennetz
collect entgegennehmen
colonial (n) Bewohner einer Kolonie
colourful farbenfroh
colourless farblos
comment (n) Kommentar
competition Konkurrenz
complaint Beschwerde
conclusion Schlußfolgerung
confidence Vertrauen
confusion Verwirrung
consider halten für
contents Inhalt
continue to fortfahren
contract Vertrag
contrast (n) Kontrast
convincing (adj) überzeugend
cookie Keks

correct sb. jmd. verbessern
corset Korsett
costume Kostüm
cottager Kleinbauer
countryman Bauer
cousin Cousin
cover (n) Einband
cow Kuh
crash (v) zerschmettern
craze (n) große Mode
creature Figur
credits Namensvorspann (beim Film)
creep (v) hereinschleichen
crew Mannschaft
crime Verbrechen
crossword (n) Kreuzworträtsel
cruel grausam
crumble (v) zusammenfallen
cry (v) schreien
crystal set Radioempfänger
cubicle kleine Zelle
cue (n) Stichwort
curl back nach oben rollen
curl up sich einrollen
curtain Vorhang
curtsey einen Knicks machen
custard pie gedeckter Kuchen mit Vanillefüllung
cut (v) schneiden
cymbal Becken

dangerous gefährlich
deaden dämpfen
death Tod

declaration Erklärung
dedication Widmung
defend verteidigen
definitive ausdrücklich
demon king böser König
describe beschreiben
despite trotz
destroy zerstören
detail (n) Einzelheit
determined entschieden
die sterben
different from anders als
difficulty Schwierigkeit
dignity Würde
dip sheep Schafe durch ein Tauchbad waschen
direction Regie
director Regisseur
disadvantage Nachteil
disappear verschwinden
disappointed (be) enttäuscht sein
disappointment Enttäuschung
disaster Katastrophe
disgraced (be) beschämt sein
disgust Abscheu
dissatisfaction Unzufriedenheit
distract ablenken
divide teilen
divine göttlich
do one's part seinen Anteil übernehmen
do without auskommen ohne
doorstep Türschwelle
doubt (n) Zweifel

dove Taube
down for (be) geplant für
drawers Unterhosen
dramatist Dramatiker
drawing room Salon
dream (n) Traum
dress (v) ankleiden
dress suit Abendanzug
dressing room Ankleideraum
drizzle (v) nieseln
drug addict Drogenabhängiger
drugstore Drogerie (mit Imbiß)
drumstick Trommelstock
due to zuzuschreiben
duke Herzog

earn verdienen
easy leicht
echo (v) widergeben
educated (adj) gebildet
effect Auswirkung
efficiency Tüchtigkeit
effort to (make) Anstrengung unternehmen
either ... or ... entweder ... oder
elongated aufgeschossen
emotion Gefühl
employ anstellen
employment Arbeit
empty (adj) leer
encourage ermutigen
enemy Feind
engage engagieren
enormous ungeheuer

entertainment Unterhaltung
enthusiastic begeisternd
enticement Verlockung
escape entkommen
established zum festen Personal gehörend
even fewer sogar weniger
even so trotzdem
evil (n) das Böse
except that außer daß
excitement Erregung
exciting aufregend
excuse (n) Entschuldigung
excuse oneself sich entschuldigen
exotic exotisch
expect erwarten
experiment (n) Experiment
explain erklären
explanation Erklärung
exploit ausbeuten
explorer Forscher
explosion Explosion
expression Ausdruck
exquisite ausgezeichnet
extraordinary außerordentlich

face (n) Gesicht
face (v) ansehen
fact (n) tatsächlich
fact Tatsache
faint (adj) unmerklich
fair (skin) hell
fairy Fee
fall over darüber stolpern

familiar with (be) vertraut sein mit
fan (n) Fächer
far (by) bei weitem
farm (n) Bauernhof
fashionable modisch
fate Schicksal
favourite (n) Lieblingsnummer
feather Feder
feckless schwach
feeling (n) Gefühl
fellow (adj) Mit ...
female weiblich
feminine Frauen ...
few wenige
fiancee Verlobte
fire (on) brennen
fire Feuer
fist Faust
fixed scheme festgefahrenes Schema
flame (n) Flamme
flash (n) Augenblick
floor (n) Boden
follow folgen
fond of (be) mögen
footlights Rampenlichter
force (v) Zwingen
forlorn verloren
formerly frühere
fortunately glücklicherweise
foxtrot Foxtrott
fraud Betrug
frequent häufig
fresh from gerade aus
frighten erschrecken
frustration Frustration
fry braten
further (go) weiter

gallant galant
garter Hosenbandorden
generous großzügig
gentleman-like höflich
gesture Geste
ghetto Getto
giant Riese
glare (n) grelles Licht
glimpse Einblick
glue (v) ankleben
glue pot Topf mit Kleister
God forbid Gott möge das verhüten
golliwog Negerpuppe
good (no) nicht gut
good-humoured gut gelaunt
good-looking gut aussehend
goose Gans
gossip Klatsch
gown Abendkleid
graceful anmutig
grade underwear Unterwäsche sortieren
grief Kummer
grinning bone eingefrorenes Lächeln
growing hopes of wachsende Hoffnung
grown-up erwachsen

guard (n) Wärter
guess (v) raten

hand in zurückgeben
handsome hübsch
handwriting Handschrift
hang aufhängen
hangover Kater (nach Alkohol)
harassed (adj) gequält
hard-working hart arbeiten
hardly kaum
harrow (n) Egge
hat Hut
haze Nebel
headdress Kopfschmuck
heart (by) auswendig
heartless herzlos
height Höhe
hide (v) verstecken
highness (royal) königliche Hoheit
hijack entführen
hire (v) anstellen
hissing & booing Zischen und Buhen
hit Erfolgs ...
hole Loch
home-freezer Gefriertruhe
honest ehrlich
hopeful hoffnungsvoll
hospitable gastfreundlich
host (n) Gastgeber
hum (v) summen
human (adj) menschlich
humour Humor

humourless humorlos
hurry (n) Eile

illegitimate unehelich
image Bild
image-building zum Vorbild anreizend
imagination Vorstellungskraft
impatient (get) ungeduldig (werden)
improbable unwahrscheinlich
incident Ereignis
inclinations Neigungen
inconsistent unbeständig
individual (n) Individuum
inefficient untüchtig
inspiration Eingebung
intellect Geist
intellectual (n) Intellektueller
intend to beabsichtigen zu
interrupt unterbrechen
interview (n) Interview
interviewer Interviewer
investigating (n) Untersuchung
invitation Einladung

Jazz age Zeitalter des Jazz
jealousy Eifersucht
join sich anschließen
joiner Schreiner
joke Witz
judgment Urteil
jump around herumspringen
justice (do sth.) einer Sache gerecht werden

keen on wild darauf sein
key-word Schlüsselwort
kill oneself sich töten
kind (adj) freundlich
knight Ritter
knowledge Wissen

lamentable beklagenswert
large groß, weit
last (v) dauern
late (the ...) der verstorbene
laugh lachen
laughter das Lachen
lavender Lavendel
law Gesetz
layer Schicht
lean across sich lehnen über
leather-bound Leder gebunden
let (v) lassen
lights Scheinwerfer
lilac Flieder
lily Lilien
limited begrenzt
listener Zuhörer
literally buchstäblich
local (adj) örtlich
location (on) Gelände für Außenaufnahmen
lock up einschließen
long to sich danach sehnen
longer (no) nicht mehr
loose lose
loud laut
lovable liebenswert
lover Geliebter

low (voice) leise
lunatic asylum Irrenanstalt

machine-gun Maschinengewehr
magician Zauberer
maiden's blush Mixgetränk "Errötendes Mädchen"
make-up dept Schminkabteilung
male (adj) männlich
mangle (n) Wäschemangel
mannerism Affektiertheit
market place Marktplatz
master shot Breitaufnahme
masterpiece Meisterwerk
matchstick Streichholz
material (n) Material
mean-looking böse aussehend
meaningful bedeutungsvoll
medium shot Halbausschnitt
memorable erinnerungswürdig
memory Erinnerung
mention (v) erwähnen
mercy Gnade
mermaid hips Hüften einer Seejungfrau
milk melken
mirror Spiegel
miss sb vermissen
mixture Mischung
moan (v) jammern
model (v) entwerfen
modest bescheiden
monosyllabic einsilbig

monstrous monströs
mood Laune, Stimmung
moonlight Mondschein
more or less mehr oder weniger
moth Motte
mournfully traurig
moustache Lippenbart
move about auf u. abgehen, sich bewegen
movement Bewegung
movie ranch Film-Ranch
music-hall Musikhalle
musician Musiker
mustard-seed Senfkorn

nanny Amme
nasty eklig
necessary nötig
need (v) verlangen
nervousness Nervosität
nettle Nessel
news-stand Zeitungskiosk
niece Nichte
nightingale Nachtigall
noise Lärm
noisy geräuschvoll
nostrils Nasenlöcher
notice (n) Bekanntmachung
notice (take no) keine Beachtung schenken
notice (v) bemerken; feststellen
noticeable bemerkenswert
number Nummer
Oak Eiche

observation Beobachtung
observer Beobachter
obsessed with besessen von
occasion Gelegenheit
occur sich ereignen
occur to in den Sinn kommen
once upon a time es war einmal ...

opinion Meinung
order (n) Orden
ordnance depot Artilleriedepot
otherwise sonst
out of sight außer Sicht
out-of-date altmodisch
outfit Aufzug (b. Kleidung)
overnight success Erfolg über Nacht
padded gepolstert
panic (n) Panik
parallel (n) Parallele
parent Eltern
part Rolle
pass door Seitentür
patience Geduld
patiently geduldig
pattern Muster
pay cheque Gehaltsscheck
pay off sich bezahlt machen
peacock Pfau
peaseblossom Erbsenblüte
perfect (adj) vollkommen
perform auftreten (Theater)
performance Aufführung
permanent ständig

perplexed verwirrt
personality Persönlichkeit
personnel s. o. Personal ...
perspective Perspektive
petticoat ausgestellter Unterrock
photographic mem. fotografisches Gedächtnis
phrase Phrase
pictorial bildhaft
pieces (fall to) (in) Stücke (fallen)
pier Pier
pile (n) Stapel
pit (n) Graben
pity (n) Mitleid
play (n) Spiel
pleasure Vergnügen
plough (v) pflügen
plucked eyebrows gezupfte Augenbrauen
poetry Dichtung
point (n) Punkt
point (to the) genau
point to auf etw. zeigen
polished (adj) geschickt
polite höflich
pompous aufgeblasen
popular beliebt
position Stellung
post-war Nachkriegs ...
practice (in) in der Praxis
precisely genau
prepare vorbereiten
presence Gegenwart

present vorstellen
press (the) Presse
press conference Pressekonferenz
prickle (n) Kribbeln
princess Prinzessin
principal (adj) Stamm ...
print (n) Druck
prisoner Gefangener
private soldier Privatsoldat
progress vorankommen
prompt (v) soufflieren
prompter Souffleur
provincial provinziell
psychiatrist Psychiater
public (n) Publikum; Öffentlichkeit
pull ziehen
punishment Strafe

quality Qualität

rationing Rationierung
reach (v) erreichen
ready (get) sich fertig machen
realise bemerken, feststellen
reality Wirklichkeit
reason Grund
recite vortragen
refuse to sich weigern
regular regelmäßig
rehearsal Probe
rehearse proben
relative (n) Verwandter
rely on sich verlassen auf

remain bleiben
repertory Repertoire
replace ersetzen
represent darstellen
reputation Ruf
rescue (n) Rettung
respect (v) respektieren
rest Ruhe
restrained gedämpft
restriction Begrenzung
result Ergebnis
review (n) Zeitschrift; Kritiken
revue Revue
rheumatism Rheumatismus
rhyming couplet gereimter Vers
ribbon Band
rip (let it) auf vollen Touren laufen lassen
rise (v) anschwellen
risque gewagt
roar (v) brüllen
roaring 20s Wilde Zwanziger Jahre
roof Dach
routine (n) Routine
row (n) Reihe
royal königlich
royalty Tantiemen
ruin (n) Zusammenbruch
ruthless rücksichtslos

safe sicher
satisfied with zufrieden mit

scandalized empört
scene Szene
scenery Landschaft
schoolboy Schuljunge
scream (v) schreien
screenplay Bühnenstück
script Manuskript
scriptwriter der Verantwortliche für das Drehbuch
secretary Sekretär
seduce verführen
self-conscious befangen
self-employed freiberuflich
sensitive empfindlich
separate (adj) getrennt
series Serie
seriously ernsthaft
servant Diener
set (n) Apparat
set (of play) Bühnenausstattung
shabbiness Schäbigkeit
shine scheinen
shiny glänzend
shock (n) Schock
shoot (a film) filmen
shortage Kürzung
shot (n) Aufnahme
shoulder Schulter
shout rufen; schreien
shut (v) schließen
sigh (v) **seufzen**
sign (n) Zeichen
sign a contract Vertrag unterzeichnen

signal Signal
signature tune Kennmelodie
silence Ruhe; Stille
silent still
silly dumm
simple einfach
single einzel
skin Haut
skirt Rock
slapstick Klamauk
sleeve Ärmel
slip out of fortschlüpfen
slipper Pantoffel
slosh scene Schlammszene, bewerfen mit Torten u. Sahne
slow-minded langsam denkend
smell of Geruch von
smile (n) Lächeln
snobbish hochnäsig
solution Lösung
sombrero mexik. Hut
sound (n) Ton
sound engineer Toningenieur
space (n) Platz; Weltraum
speech Rede
spider Spinne
spirit Geist
spontaneous spontan
spotlight Scheinwerfer
spray (v) spritzen
staccato (n) Stakkato
stage (n) Bühne
stage-box Theaterloge
stalls Sperrsitz
stamp (v) stempeln

stamp their feet mit den Füßen trampeln
stare (n) starrer Blick
stare at starren auf
steam railway Dampflokomotive
step in dazwischentreten
steps (n) Treppe
stir (n) Unruhe
stir up aufrühren
stomach Magen
store (n) Vorrat
storm & rage stürmen und rasen
storm of applause Sturm von Applaus
strategic strategisch wichtig
straw-coloured strohfarben
street car Straßenbahnwagen
string Schnur
study (of sb.) Studie (von jem.)
style Gerstenkorn
sublime großartig
suburb Vorort
succeed Erfolg haben
success Erfolg
suffer leiden
suggest vorschlagen; anregen
suitable passend; geeignet
sunbonnet Sonnenhut (Haube)
super (adj) überragend
super-sophisticated ungeheuer erfahren
supporting actor Schauspieler in der Nebenrolle

supreme ausgezeichnet
supreme court Oberster Gerichtshof
surprising überraschend
surround umgeben
sustained gut gespielt
sweat (n) Schweiß
sweet-faced lieb
swinger lockerer Typ
swooning point Ohnmachtsanfall

tailcoats Frack
tailor Schneider
take (n) Aufnahme
talk (n) Gespräch
tap (v) klopfen
taste (n) Geschmack
teach beibringen
tear (n) Tränen
tears (near to) den Tränen nahe
temper (lose) Geduld verlieren
tenant-farmer Gutspächter
tension Spannung
terrorize in Schrecken versetzen
theatre-goer Theaterbesucher
theatrical Theater ...
thin dünn
thinly dürftig
thought (n) Gdanke
thrilling (adj) aufregend
throne Trohn
throw werfen
tie (n) Krawatte

tiger rag Titel eines Songs
timeless zeitlos
timing zeitliche Abstimmung
tinker Kesselflicker
tip-up seat Klappsitz
tired müde
title song Titelsong
titter kichern
tolerant tolerant
tombstone Grabsteine
top hat Zylinderhut
topic Thema
touch (v) berühren
tough hart
trail (v) hinter sich herziehen
treatment Behandlung
trick (n) Trick
triumphant triumphierend
trivial (adj) banal
troupe Gruppe
trunks kurze Hose
truth Wahrheit
tune Melodie
tuneful melodiös
turn away ablehnen; abweisen
turn to sb. sich an jem. wenden
tyrant Tyrann

ugly häßlich
uncomfortable unbequem
uncommon ungewöhnlich
uncritical unkritisch
understudy als Ersatzmann spielen
unhospital-like ungastlich

unimaginable nicht vorstellbar
unique einzigartig
unjustified ungerechtfertigt
unknown unbekannt
unopened ungeöffnet
unreserved nicht reserviert
unsolved (adj) ungelöst
unsophisticated unerfahren
upper lip Oberlippe
used (adj) abgetragen

variable unterschiedlich
variety theatre Varietétheater
veil (n) Schleier
venetian venezianisch
vice-chancellor Vizekanzler
victim Opfer
village green Dorfplatz

walk (n) Gang
wallpaper paste Tapetenkleister
wand Zauberstab
ward (n) Schützling
wardrobe Garderobe
washbasin Waschbecken
washing line Wäscheleine
washing machine Waschmaschine
washing-up machine Geschirrspüler

waste (time) Zeit vergeuden
waste of time Zeitverschwendung
watch for aufpassen
wave (v) winken
way (be under) vorangehen
weak schwach
weaver Weber
wedding day Hochzeitstag
well-known berühmt
well-tried ermüdend
western Western (Film)
whatever was auch immer
wherever wo auch immer
whistle pfeifen
whoever wer auch immer
wholly vollkommen
widow's kiss Witwenkuß (Name eines Cocktails)
wild about verrückt sein nach
willing gewillt
wit Witz
women's institute Traueninstitut
wood Wald
woodcutter Holzfäller
worry (n) Sorge
worry (v) sich sorgen

yawn (n) Gähnen

Zig-Zag (adj) Zickzack ...